THE
CANADIAN
ROCKIES

AN **ARiEL** BOOK

The CANADIAN ROCKIES

The Summit of Mt. Resplendent

Seen from above, the mountain parks are craggy landscapes
composed largely of barren, inhabitable rock. The frozen
summit of Mount Resplendent, although beautiful, is a
desolate and forbidding place in the winter.

left
Yellow Orchids

Alpine meadows are afire with the colours of wild flowers
in the summer months. The yellow lady's slipper is a
woodland plant with a long, graceful stem and
slipper-like pouch lined with purple streaks.
It grows best in moist, shady areas at low elevations,
and is the most scented of the orchid family.

WATERTON

left
Waterton Lakes National Park
Established in 1932 as an International Peace Park, Waterton shares its upper lake with Glacier National Park in Montana. Rising abruptly from the plains, these front range mountains were formed relatively recently, when 1.5 million-year-old sediment came to rest atop much younger shales. Thus, Waterton's mountains are, in fact, upside down.

Cameron Falls
Immediately beneath the turbulent waters of Cameron Falls is the oldest visible rock in the Rockies. Located near the townsite, the falls are a highlight of Waterton Lakes National Park.

KANANASKIS & CANMORE

The Three Sisters
Unofficially called Faith, Hope and Charity, the Three Sisters are Canmore's signature mountains. The site of the 1988 Winter Olympic Games, Canmore's Nordic Centre features 56 km of cross country ski trails which are a playground for mountain bikers in the summer months.

left
King Canyon—Kananaskis Country
The montane forest and grassland of King Canyon are typical of this area. K-Country contains three provincial parks, and is a popular destination for hikers, skiers, boaters, campers and cyclists. As it sustains a variety of wildlife, sightings of grazers such as elk and moose, as well as of their predators, are common.

BANFF

Banff

Located in the heart of the Rockies, Banff is a
world famous destination where nature meets
culture. It is both a meeting ground for
mountaineers and, with its Centre of Fine Arts,
museums and galleries, it forms the cultural
nexus of the Bow Valley.

right
Cascade Mountain

Cascade Mountain forms the northern
backdrop for the town of Banff. Between 1903
and 1922, during which 55 km (34 mi) of coal
tunnels were excavated, a mining town called
Bankhead flourished at its base. Traces of the
mines still remain. Visitors can access
Bankhead and get a closer view of Castle
Mountain on the C-level Cirque
interpretive trail.

overleaf
Mount Rundle

Mount Rundle rises like the crest of a stone
wave over the Bow Valley. Nestled in its wake
are the Banff Springs Hotel and the Banff
Centre for the Arts. Named after a Methodist
missionary to the natives of the Northwest, its
imposing height 2846 m (9337 feet)
makes it a well-known landmark.

BANFF

Banff Springs Hotel in Winter
Bruce Price was commissioned by the CPR to design
a hotel which, when it opened in 1888, was the largest in
the world. Its chateau style, in keeping with late Victorian
architecture, became highly influential in Canada, and is
the predominant form for government buildings.

right
Banff Springs Hotel
William Cornelius Van Horne, General Manager of the
CPR, knew that in order to attract visitors to
the Rockies, the Banff Springs Hotel had to be the epitome
of elegant luxury. Today, its world famous golf course,
swimming pool, fine restaurants and lovely suites are
evidence of his success in realizing this vision.

BANFF

Hoodoo

The Tunnel Mountain Hoodoo Trail leads directly to these eerie figures which Stoney natives believed were the teepees of "bad gods." Hoodoos form when capstones protect the material directly beneath them from erosion, while the surrounding material is weathered away.

right
Bow Falls

Following the Bow River from Banff townsite is a trail which leads to the falls. The Bow River derives its name from the Cree words meaning "the place from which bows are taken," as its banks support saplings which were fashioned by natives into hunting bows.

BANFF

Sulphur Mountain Summit

An exquisite view of the Bow Valley unfolds
in the eight minutes it takes to ride the gondola
2285 m (7497 ft) to the top of Sulphur
Mountain. Bighorn sheep abound at the
summit, and will readily approach
curious visitors.

right
Bow Valley and Golf Course

The Banff Springs golf course is rated among
the ten most scenic links in the world. Elk and
mule deer have been known to watch curiously
from the edge of the green as visitors, taking in
the mountain air, participate in this game.

BANFF

Johnston's Canyon

Johnston's Canyon is one of the most interesting and accessible hikes in the mountain parks. A walkway built into the canyon leads into its depths, providing a splendid view of seven churning waterfalls. Six km (3.7 mi) from the trailhead are the blue-green inkpots, endlessly percolating a sediment which resembles quicksand.

right
Castle Mountain

This aptly named castellated mountain was formed with the erosion of the weak layers of shale which originally separated more resistant limestone formations. The towers and stairs that remain give Castle Mountain the chiselled appearance to which it owes its name.

WILDLIFE

Grey Wolf

Portrayed for centuries as a bloodthirsty and evil trickster,
the grey or timber wolf displays such human characteristics
as pair bonding and sharing. This largest wild member of
the dog family has one of the most sophisticated social
orders of any mammal.

left
Bald Eagle

Benjamin Franklin lamented the choice of the bald eagle as
the U.S. national emblem, claiming that it was "of bad
moral character" and lived by "sharping and robbing."
While it patrols riverbanks and lake shores to scavenge for
dead fish and animal remains, it also pursues live rabbits,
full-grown waterfowl and young goats or sheep.

KOOTENAY

Radium Hot Springs

When water filters through cracks in the earth's surface
and approaches the warmer core, it is heated. Gathering
minerals along its route, it resurfaces to form a thermal
spring. Early mountaineers believed, as did the Romans,
that a soak in the hot mineral springs had healing powers.

left
Marble Canyon

Glacier-chilled air envelops the interpretive trail leading
over Tokumm Creek and into Marble Canyon. As a result,
the lower subalpine canyon forest in this area supports
many species of vegetation normally found in the arctic.
The glacial silt in the water polishes the canyon walls,
producing a marble-like finish.

MORAINE LAKE

Moraine Lake
Samuel Allen named the peaks behind Moraine Lake in 1893, after
the Stoney words for the numbers one to ten. The Valley of the Ten
Peaks has since been named Wenkchemna Valley—the Stoney word
for "ten." The icy source that feeds the lake is Wenkchemna Glacier,
concealed from view at the mountain's north side.

left
Bull Elk
Elk are also known as Wapiti, the Shawnee Native word for "white
rump." Elk stags have massive, branching antlers which they shed
and grow back, each year acquiring a larger rack. Sparring for mates
occurs during the fall rut, when they announce their presence by
bugling, squealing and barking at their opponents.

preceding
Moraine Lake
Assuming that the lake was dammed by a glacial moraine,
Walter Wilcox named it Moraine Lake in 1899. Sedimentary rock
deposits which originally lay on the floor of a shallow inland sea
form a rockpile on one shore. This rockslide debris provides an
alternative explanation for the lake's original dam.

LAKE LOUISE

Lake Louise

Stoney natives described this place to early mountaineers as
"the big snow mountain above the lake of little fishes."
Today, visitors can rent paddle boats to explore the lake,
and may even see beavers swimming or feeding
close to the shore.

left
Chateau Lake Louise

In 1890, the CPR built a chalet on the lake shore that was
to develop into the Chateau Lake Louise. Originally built to
promote the new railway line, it has blossomed from a
tiny log cabin into the luxury hotel
that today houses 1000 guests.

LAKE LOUISE

Mt. Temple

Mt. Temple is the highest peak in the Lake
Louise area, standing 3,543 m (11,624 ft) above
sea level. Walter Wilcox and Samuel Allen
first climbed it in 1894, at which time it was
the only Canadian mountain over 3,353 m
(11,000 ft) to be summited.

right
Lake Louise Trail

Starting in front of the Chateau, the Lake
Louise trail winds its way along the lake before
climbing gently. It branches in two directions:
toward the teahouse below the Plain of Six
Glaciers, or to Agnes Lake and its teahouse.
Visitors who would like an alternative to
hiking can make their way along the trail
on horseback.

overleaf
Lake Louise Poppies

On the slopes of Mt. Victoria is the
Plain of Six Glaciers. The scars or moraines
which the glaciers have etched out record their
advance and retreat. Down below, in the
glacier-cooled wind, Icelandic poppies thrive.
Although they are far from home, these
Siberian natives have found ideal conditions
on the banks of Lake Louise.

YOHO

Natural Bridge

The Kicking Horse River carves its way through weak
shales until it meets Natural Bridge. Stubbornly, this
resistant outcrop of limestone stands its ground. Over the
years, it has compromised somewhat, bearing a downward
crack or "bridge" through which the river gushes.

left
Beaver

An ally to conservationists, "nature's lumberjack" creates
dams that help control flooding. The beaver must gnaw or
die, as its constantly growing incisors would otherwise curve
inward and pierce its skull. It is slow and clumsy on land
but agile under water, and can hold its breath for up to 15
minutes or breathe trapped air bubbles
under winter ice.

YOHO

Emerald Lake
Emerald Lake, the largest in Yoho, is a favourite destination
of avid hikers. Its lodge is constructed on a glacial moraine,
and is the starting point for hikes along the shoreline or
toward the glacial amphitheatre of Emerald Basin.

right
Takakkaw Falls
Takakkaw is a Cree word meaning "it is magnificent." These
falls, which are the emblem of Yoho National Park, are fed
by a lake at the toe of Daly Glacier.
In the winter, the volume of glacial runoff
is reduced to a trickle.

WILDLIFE

Black Bear Cubs

Black bear cubs are born in January and February, and
usually spend their first 16 months with their mother. They
are found in heavily forested areas, and are strong
swimmers and tree climbers. In Banff and Jasper National
Parks, black bears are outnumbered 2:1 by their only
natural enemy: the grizzly.

left
Grizzly

The largest and most powerful carnivore in the Rockies,
the grizzly can range from creamy yellow to black in
colour. These elusive loners are most often found in upper
alpine meadows. While 90% of the grizzly's diet is
composed of vegetable matter, it also preys on ungulates,
small mammals and even grizzly cubs.

Herbert Lake

A tarn, of which Herbert Lake is a fine example, is formed by the effects of a glacier's movement. Such lakes are either depressions gouged out of the bedrock, or meltwater that is dammed by glacial rubble or moraine.

left
Crowfoot Glacier

Crowfoot Glacier illustrates the story of its own formation. The steep upper cliffs deposit snow on the lower slopes, which then turns to glacial ice in the shady or lee side of Crowfoot Mountain. Over time, the glacier retreats, etching out the mountain's features.

Golden Mantled Ground Squirrel

Identified by the black and white stripe that extends from shoulder
to rump and the golden cloak that covers its head and shoulders, this
variety of ground squirrel eats seeds, berries and insects to store fat
for its winter hibernation. It makes its home in the rocky
regions of alpine and subalpine zones.

left
Bow Lake

The principal source of the Bow River is the glacier-fed Bow Lake.
In 1920, Jimmy Simpson built a mountaineering cabin on the lake
shore, which he expanded when the Icefields Parkway was built
in the 30s. This log cabin was the forerunner of the beautiful
Num-ti-Jah Lodge which stands in its place today.

overleaf
Peyto Lake Sunrise

"Wild" Bill Peyto was an English immigrant who, soon after his
arrival in 1890, adapted to his new life as a trail guide in the rugged
backcountry. He guided many expeditions, among which was the
discovery of the Columbia Icefield in 1898. He later became one of
the first park wardens. Peyto Lake Overlook offers one of
the most spectacular views in the park.

ICEFIELD PARKWAY

Snocoach Tour

The safest and most interesting way to discover the Columbia Icefields is on a Brewster Snocoach tour, where experienced guides reveal the mysteries of this vast, frozen landscape.

left
Athabasca Glacier

Both Athabasca Glacier's close proximity to the Icefields Parkway and the Forefield Trail which accesses it make this glacier the most accessible one in North America. Athabasca is one of eight outlet valley glaciers that flow from Columbia Icefield. Hikers should bundle up to explore this area; very little of the snow that falls here melts, and the wind coming off the ice is chilly.

ICEFIELD PARKWAY

Sunwapta Falls
A glacial moraine has diverted the Sunwapta River
from its former course, causing it to force its way through
the limestone bedrock. Having created a steep canyon,
the water tumbles down Sunwapta Falls before
rejoining the Athabasca River.

left
Athabasca Falls
The Athabasca Falls cascade over a step in the underlying
bedrock. The durable Gog quartzite of which it is made
resisted glacial erosion, and continues to hold up under the
persistent rush of water. Fenced viewpoints at the top of the
falls overlook the water's 23 m (76 ft) plunge
to the valley bottom below.

JASPER

Jasper Tramway

The 937 m (3074 ft) climb of the Jasper
Tramway offers an inspiring view of the
Athabasca and Miette River valleys.
Spanning montane, subalpine and alpine
ecoregions, a ride on the tramway is a
unique and exciting experience.

right
Mt. Edith Cavell

Edith Louisa Cavell, an English nurse who was
executed by the Germans for assisting the
escape of Allied prisoners of war during WWI,
is this mountain's namesake. Less than 100
years ago, Angel Glacier retreated to merge
with Cavell Glacier. The marks of its movement
can be seen from the path of the Glacier trail.

JASPER

Jasper Park Lodge
Because the town of Jasper grew rapidly after the CPR was built, a "tent city" was erected on the shore of Lac Beauvert. This need to accommodate the rapid influx of visitors gave rise to the construction of the Jasper Park Lodge.

opposite
Lac Beauvert
The French name of this horseshoe shaped lake refers to its beautiful green colour. It is not the water itself, however, that is green. Rather, the silt or material at the bottom that was ground by a glacier's passing reflects light in a particular way, making the lake appear coloured.

Pika
The pika or "rock rabbit" changes its camouflage to match the rocks in its surroundings.

JASPER

Mountain Goat
More closely related to Asian antelopes than to goats, this nimble climber is found in the rugged terrain above 2,000 m (6,500 ft). It is ideally suited to its harsh environment, growing a warm beard and chaps on its front legs in winter. Its pliable hooves act both as suction cups and shock absorbers, allowing it to manoeuvre on steep cliffs.

right:
Pyramid Mountain
Less than 10 km from Jasper townsite stands Pyramid Mountain. Its reddish face is reflected in the serene waters of Patricia Lake. Princess Patricia, daughter of Canada's Governor General from 1911–1916, is its namesake.

JASPER

Maligne Lake Sunrise

Known as "Chaba Imne" or Beaver Lake by the Stoneys,
Maligne Lake is the largest natural body of water in the
Rockies. In 1846, a Jesuit missionary who had trouble
crossing the river near its mouth gave it the
French name Maligne: Wicked.

left:
Maligne Canyon

An early visitor to this site commented that, compared to
this largest and deepest of the Rockies' limestone canyons,
"any other is like a crack in a teacup." From the teahouse at
the top, visitors can explore the canyon that Maligne River
has etched out over the course of 11,000 years.

JASPER

Roche Miette

"Miette"—the French word for crumb—is not a particularly
apt name for this mountain, as it is composed of one of the
tougher limestones. It was more likely named in honour of a
19th century fur trader named Miette who, it is said,
ascended the mountain and dangled his legs over the edge
when he reached the summit.

left
Maligne Lake

Glacial meltwater from the Brazeau Icefield collects in the
lake and in turn feeds Maligne River, which follows a major
fault line in the earth's crust. The valley contains an
underground river system which stretches for 17 km,
and may be the largest in the world.

MOUNT ROBSON

Mount Robson Provincial Park

British Columbia's Mount Robson is the highest peak in the entire range. Also
called "Cloud Cap Mountain," the summit of this giant is a rare sight indeed.
One of the most spectacular glacier systems in the Rockies is hidden from view
on Robson's north side; to behold it is the backpacker's hard-earned reward.

Canadian Cataloguing in Publication Data
Grobler, Sabrina, 1972-
Canadian Rockies

ISBN 1-55153-828-8

1. Rocky Mountains, Canadian (B.C. and Alta.)--Pictorial works.* 2. Rocky
Mountains, Canadian (B.C. and Alta.)* I. Title
FC219.G76 1997   971.1'0022'2   C96-910877-X
F1080.G76 1997
Copyright © 1997 Altitude Publishing Canada Ltd.

Photographs: Carole Harmon, Don Harmon, Stephen Hutchings,
Dennis and Esther Schmidt, Doug Leighton p.11, Chris Dunlop p. 7

Production:

Art Direction and Design	Stephen Hutchings
Project management	Sharon Komori
Production management	Mark Higenbottam
Financial management	Laurie Smith
Sales management	Scott Davidson

A participant in the Altitude GreenTree Program in which twice as many trees
will be planted as were used in the manufacturing of this book.

Printed in Canada by Friesen Printers, Altona Manitoba

Ariel Publishing
1500 Railway Avenue, Canmore Alberta T1W 1P6
(403) 678-8888 • Order Desk 1-800-957-6888